WAKE UP! IT'S TIME TO DREAM

A guide through the crossroads into
the life your dream already knows

KIRAN RYAN-YOUNG

Published with the assistance of Tarafied Publishing
https://www.tarafiedpublishing.com/

Paperback ISBN: 979-8-9931384-0-4
Ebook ISBN: 979-8-9931384-1-1

Cover design & Interior layout by Asya Blue Design
Edited by Tara Hayes
Developmental editing by Dr. Anne Bartolucci

This is a work of nonfiction. References to public figures are for illustrative purposes only and do not imply endorsement.

For permissions, inquiries, or bulk orders, contact:
kiran@amilliondreamers.com

Printed in the United States of America.

For my mother,

You always told me I should write a book. I didn't believe you at the time, but you kept saying it like you knew something I didn't. Turns out, you were right. I started writing this while you were still here. Then you were gone. Finishing it felt harder than I imagined. I kept going because you believed in me. Because I could still hear your voice. Because this dream started with you. I miss you every day. This book exists because of you. It carries your spirit, your values, your dreams. And it's one more way I get to say thank you.

For my daughter, Zelia,

You are my greatest dream come true. From the moment you arrived, you changed the way I see the world and the way I see myself. You remind me to stay curious, to be bold, and to lead with love. So much of Grand Mère lives in you. Her strength, her sparkle, her sense of joy. And so much is uniquely, beautifully your own. Watching you grow has helped me grow, too. Thank you for choosing me. I am endlessly proud to be your Papa. Keep becoming. The world needs what only you can give.

"All our dreams can come true, if we have the courage to pursue them." [1]

—Walt Disney

1 Walt Disney, *The Quotable Walt Disney*. Disney Editions, 2001

CONTENTS

"When everything falls apart and the world finally goes quiet, your dream won't shout, it'll whisper. And if you're still enough, you'll hear it calling you back to yourself."

—Kiran

INTRODUCTION

THE PAUSE

What was your big dream as a child?

Did you dream of driving the fastest race car and winning every race in the world? Were you part of a singing group, rehearsing routines in your living room, preparing to go on tour? Maybe you were a circus performer riding elephants under the big top or a baseball player hitting the game-winning home run. Perhaps you imagined yourself traveling the world with a passport full of stamps, starring on television, or running your own candy business.

As children, we were able to dream freely. We could imagine worlds, tell fantastical stories, and believe anything was possible. Then one day, out of nowhere, someone who thought they were doing us a favor told us that we had to be "realistic." There is no place in the real world for dreams. Dreaming's for kids.

We believed them, and we stopped.

We traded in those big, audacious, technicolor dreams for a smaller vision of life filled with checklists and expectations, "should's" and "supposed to's." We chose survival over passion, certainty over curiosity.

And yet, no matter how much we pushed them aside, our dreams never left us. Our dreams are stronger than that. Once they have found us, they will never let us go.

Dreaming isn't optional. It's not just for kids or the privileged few who have time, money, and freedom. It's not a luxury for when life slows down, when the timing is right, when we've checked all the responsibility boxes.

Dreaming is necessary for all.

Dreams make up who we are.

Dreams are how new ideas are born, how change happens, how we step into the life we're meant to create. Our dream isn't just for us; it has the power to impact others.

So, I ask you, "Are you ready and willing to reclaim your big, audacious, technicolor dreams?"

Owning My Dream: The Story That Changed Everything

For years, I carried a dream so audacious, so seemingly impossible, that I barely let myself believe in it. I wanted to be a parent. Not in some distant, hypothetical future, but truly, deeply—I wanted to raise a child, to love them, to guide them, to witness the world through their eyes.

This was a burning need that wouldn't let go, even when fear told me my dream was impossible. I worried that it was too big, too impractical, and too far out of reach for someone like me.

I didn't know how it would happen or if it even *could* happen. As a gay man in the mid-80s and 90s, the idea of fatherhood wasn't just unconventional; it was nearly unimaginable. There were no roadmaps, no easy paths. Adoption wasn't a viable option for me at the time, and surrogacy was barely a whisper of a possibility. Society had a script, and my dream didn't fit neatly into its pages. So, my dream got pushed aside.

Fifteen years later, the dream seized its opportunity to be seen again. To be heard. I listened and I said yes. Out loud.

The first person I shared this dream with was my cousin Davina. She had gone through her own difficult journey to become a parent. She wanted children, but her husband did not. When they divorced, she saw an opportunity to pursue what had always been in her heart. After much thought, she decided to have a child on her own through artificial insemination. It was a bold choice for a woman at the time. Not just to raise a baby solo, but to do so using a method that was still unfamiliar and misunderstood by many.

There were many ups and downs along the way. I remember her telling me about the process: choosing a donor, visiting with doctors, preparing for the baby's arrival, even considering possible names. Every part of her journey was deliberate, courageous, and filled with intention. Watching her speak her dream aloud and see it through gave me the space and courage to speak mine.

And I did. For the first time, I shared my dream of being a parent with someone. (Big exhale.) That moment changed everything.

Once the words were out in the world, it was like a door had opened. A door I hadn't even known was there. My cousin, Davina, offered to have a baby for me.

This selfless act of love was the response to me proclaiming my dream. Her commitment to go on the journey with me filled my heart and fueled my dream. I could no longer just think the dream to myself; I had to claim it. I had to do more than just wish. I said yes, and in that moment, I chose to own the dream.

Two years later, on my first date with Timm, the man who would become my husband, I spoke my dream again. I asked him if he wanted children. Without hesitation, he said yes. And with that, my dream moved one step closer to becoming reality. Speaking your dream out loud, claiming it with intention and commitment, makes all the difference.

With their support and unwavering belief in me, my dream was achieved. In 2006, I became a parent. My dream came to life, not because it was handed to me, but because I claimed it, shared it, and pursued it with everything I had, no matter how audacious or impractical it may have seemed. And it changed me.

I share this not because my story is extraordinary, but because it isn't. We all have dreams that seem just out of reach. We all carry visions that we hesitate to claim.

No matter how much we push them aside, no matter how much time has passed, they wait for us. They whisper to us in the quiet moments. They resurface when we least expect them. Because they are part of us.

The Pause and the Whisper

The pause is when something stops you in your tracks. Sometimes you choose it, but more often, it chooses you.

A layoff. A birth. A goodbye. A child leaving for college. A wedding vow. A whispered "I'm done."

Sometimes it's a crisis. Sometimes it arrives quietly, wrapped in joy or change. But no matter how it comes, the pause breaks your rhythm and leaves you breathless.

You realize that your life up to this point is over. The chapter has closed, and what's ahead hasn't yet begun.

It's disorienting, this interruption, a stillness you didn't ask for. But in that quiet, something stirs.

Pause.

Take a breath.

Do you hear it? That quiet voice in the back of your mind? The one that's been there for years, waiting for you to listen?

That whisper is your dream.

For some, it's an old dream buried beneath responsibilities, set aside in favor of practicality. For others, it's a new idea, something stirring just beneath the surface, asking for your attention.

Either way, it's easy to ignore. To tell yourself this is not the right time. To believe that maybe you're too late.

But you're not. Because in the space the pause creates, a new question forms:

What now?

Not a question of duty, expectation, or routine, but one that's raw, honest, and authentically yours.

The pause doesn't demand an answer. It offers an opening. A threshold. A door you didn't know existed.

And though you may not have asked for it, the pause gives you something sacred:

Permission.

Permission to come home to yourself. Permission to listen more deeply. Permission to be open to the dreams that have been whispering to you all along. Permission to want more. Permission to dream again.

> ★ **Wake-up call**
> Your dreams don't expire. They wait. For this moment.

The Journey We're Taking Together

This book isn't about waiting for the right moment or hoping passively for a change.

This book is about waking up. It's about recognizing the dream that's been calling you, giving yourself permission to pursue it, and taking action despite uncertainty.

You will receive **Wake-Up Calls** throughout the book. These are truths to guide you through this dream journey, nudges, reminders, and moments of clarity designed to keep you connected to what matters most.

Together, we'll explore:

- The different types of dreams and which one is worth committing to (Spoiler: it's your Life Dream).

- How to move past fear, self-doubt, and the belief that it's too late.

- Why action, not just vision, is what turns dreams into reality.

- The power of surrounding yourself with the right people.

- How to create momentum and persevere, even when things get tough.

By the end, you'll move past inspiration into action.

It's Time to Wake Up

So, let's pause.

Take a breath.

Listen.

Because right now, in this moment, you're standing at the edge of something new.

And the only question is:

Are you ready to wake up and dream?

"The first yes has to come from you, because no one else can give it. That's where the dream begins."

—Kiran

SECTION ONE

. . . .

PERMISSION GRANTED

CHAPTER 1

YOUR DREAM DATE – CHOOSING THE DREAM THAT STAYS

I f dreams were people, what kind would you choose to be in a long-term relationship with?

Some dreams are thrilling but unpredictable. Others charm you with endless possibilities but never commit. And then, there's the one: the dream that sticks around, challenges you, and pushes you to grow.

In this chapter, we're meeting your three potential dream dates and deciding which one is worth pursuing.

The Three Types of Dreams

Dream #1: Night Dream – The Mysterious Stranger

Night Dream is the kind of date who sweeps you off your feet, takes you on a wild adventure, and then disappears the morning after. One night, they have you flying over a city; the next, you're trapped in a high school exam for a class you never took. Exciting? Sure. Reliable? Not at all.

Even so, this type of dream serves a purpose. Night Dreams help us process emotions and solve problems, and they occasionally spark creative ideas (fun fact: Paul McCartney's song *Yesterday* and Mary Shelley's *Frankenstein* were both inspired by dreams).

Sometimes, Night Dreams can be sacred meeting places where we reunite with those no longer around in body but still deeply present in spirit. My mother visited me in a dream a few weeks after she passed. We had coffee, we talked, she smiled. She had the most contagious smile. Even just thinking about that dream, that visit, makes me smile. It was brief but perfect. It felt like a big hug. It was a gift to experience a presence full of comfort and love.

As powerful as they can be, Night Dreams fade with the morning light. They're fleeting visitors, leaving behind impressions, insights, and sometimes healing, but rarely staying long enough to build something lasting. They pass through, often without warning, leaving you to ponder their meaning and significance.

Verdict: Fleeting, mysterious, and sometimes unforgettable.

Have you ever woken up from a dream with a smile that lingered all day, even knowing the moment you dreamed up will never reoccur?

Dream #2: Daydream – The Charming but Noncommittal Romantic

You know that person who has big ideas but never follows through? That's Daydream.

Daydream slips in when there is little competition. When you're bored, resting, or just looking out the window. There's nothing to distract you. Those moments when your mind is not fully engaged but totally free to wander. That's when Daydream shows up on your doorstep, ready to show you anything your heart desires: living in a villa in Tuscany, giving a TED Talk, or accepting an Oscar. With Daydream, everything seems possible. Daydream fills your mind with what-ifs and could-be's.

And then? They disappear.

Daydreams are wonderful for sparking creativity and possibility, but they rarely move past the imagining stage. They're the kind of date who plans an elaborate cross-country road trip but never actually books the car.

I have daydreams about skydiving all the time. The views are incredible; I love the feeling of flying in the air. I also love the fact that I never have to actually do it.

Verdict: Inspiring, exciting, but unreliable.

Have you ever felt the excitement of a daydream only to find yourself hesitating or stuck when it came time to act?

Dream #3: Life Dream – The One Worth Committing To

Now, meet Life Dream, the dream that sticks around.

Like my dream of becoming a parent, Life Dream doesn't just talk about what could be; they push you to make it happen, even if you push back. They challenge you, excite you, and sometimes even scare you. But they're here for the long haul.

These are the dreams that shape your life: starting a business, writing a book, launching a creative project, and making an impact. They demand your attention, energy, and effort. Unlike Night Dream and Daydream, Life Dream needs action.

★ **Wake-Up Call**
You already have a Life Dream. Maybe it's been whispering to you for years, waiting for you to listen. Maybe it's evolved over time. Or maybe, just maybe, you've been afraid to admit how much you want it.

"Has there ever been a dream so important that just thinking about it made your heart race and your pulse quicken?"

How They Work Together

While these three types of dreams may seem separate, they actually work together in powerful ways.

- **Night Dreams** can be a source of comfort and inspiration, giving us fresh ideas and perspectives we may not have considered in waking life. Many artists, scientists, and innovators have credited Night Dreams with sparking their breakthroughs. Some say that Albert Einstein's theory of relativity was influenced by a dream about cows being electrocuted!

- **Daydreams** serve as the bridge between fantasy and reality. They help us explore possibilities without pressure. That daydream about moving to another country or starting a nonprofit? It's planting the seed, testing the waters, and helping you envision a different life.

- **Life Dreams** take those seeds and help them blossom into real-world action. They require commitment, resilience, and courage. You may daydream about writing a book, but the moment you sit down and put words on the page, you begin the journey of turning that Daydream into a Life Dream.

Rather than dismissing Night Dreams and Daydreams, recognize them as part of the creative process. They are stepping stones to something greater, helping you refine your vision and fuel your pursuit of the Life Dream that matters most.

The Scenic Route (Where Magic Meets the Mess)

"Success is sometimes the outcome of a whole string of failures." [2]

—Vincent van Gogh

Let's be real. Saying yes to a Life Dream isn't always easy. It can be scary. It means journeying into uncharted territory without a perfect roadmap. Some days, you'll feel unstoppable. Other days, you'll wonder if you're crazy for even trying. You might face setbacks, doubts, and unexpected challenges. That's normal.

Even Walt Disney, whose name is now synonymous with creativity and success, was once told he lacked imagination. Before he built an empire, he faced rejection, bankruptcy, and failure. But he kept going because his Life Dream was worth it.

---

2 Vincent van Gogh, *The Letters of Vincent van Gogh*, ed. Mark Roskill (New York Graphic Society, 1963), 56.

Many others have encountered major obstacles:

- **The Wright Brothers** were mocked for their belief that humans could fly. They faced financial struggles, public skepticism, and multiple failed prototypes before successfully launching the first powered flight in 1903.
- **Oprah Winfrey** was told she wasn't fit for television.
- **Steven Spielberg** was rejected from film school more than once before becoming one of the most influential directors in history.

Sometimes we're the ones getting in our own way. Pursuing a Life Dream means encountering resistance, not just from the world, but from yourself. Self-doubt, fear of failure, and unexpected setbacks will test your resolve. Dreams evolve, shift, and sometimes take detours, but individuals who persist are the ones who make those dreams a reality.

The key is to be willing to keep moving forward.

DREAMER SPOTLIGHT: WALT DISNEY
(Animator, Visionary, Entrepreneur)
Bringing Imagination to Life

. . . .

*"The way to get started is to quit talking
and begin doing."* [3]

—Walt Disney

One of the most repeated stories about Walt Disney is that
a newspaper editor once fired him, claiming he "lacked
imagination and had no good ideas."

That didn't stop him.

Disney went on to create Mickey Mouse, Disneyland,
and a legacy of storytelling that has shaped generations.
Beyond making cartoons, his Life Dream was to create a
world of magic, adventure, and wonder.

But even Disney faced moments of uncertainty. Before
the success of Mickey Mouse, he lost the rights to his
first major character, Oswald the Lucky Rabbit. Disney
saw this setback as an opportunity to dream bigger. His
resilience and commitment to his vision turned adversity
into the foundation of something greater.

★ **Wake-Up Call**
Setbacks don't define us; our response to them does.

---

3 Walt Disney, *The Quotable Walt Disney* (Disney Editions, 2001).

Dream Activation Exercise: Recognizing the Dreams Within You

You have a Life Dream, whether you've fully acknowledged it or not. Let's take the first step in bringing it into focus.

Reflection Questions:

1. What's a dream that has stuck with you over time, something you've thought about again and again?

2. What's something you've imagined yourself doing that excites you, even if it scares you?

3. If there were no obstacles, if success were guaranteed, what dream would you pursue?

4. What small step can you take this week to move toward that dream?

5. Think about a moment in your life when you felt truly alive. What were you doing, and how does it connect to your dreams?

Write down your answers. These are the whispers of your Life Dream.

And guess what? It's time to stop ignoring them.

Final Thoughts: Who's Your Dream Date?

So, who are you choosing?

Night Dream is exciting but unreliable. Daydream is charming but inconsistent. But Life Dream?

Life Dream is ready when you are.

This book is your guide to making that commitment, to stop thinking about your dreams and start living them.

Your Life Dream is waiting.

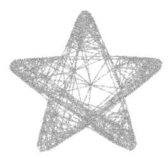

CHAPTER 2

GIVING YOURSELF PERMISSION TO DREAM

Someone once said to you, "That's sweet, but be realistic." Can you remember how quickly excitement turned to embarrassment or doubt?

In the introduction, we discussed how dreams are often pushed aside for practicality, and in Chapter 1, we explored the importance of dreams. But even when you've identified your Life Dream, fully embracing it requires your own permission.

We like to believe that dreaming is natural, that when inspiration strikes, we'll simply step into our vision without hesitation. But for many of us, the hardest part isn't having a dream; it's believing we're worthy of it.

Perhaps you've dismissed your dream as impractical, convinced yourself that now isn't the right time, or worried that it's selfish to want more. Maybe you've been waiting for someone else's approval to validate your dream, grant you permission, and reassure you, "Yes, you're allowed to want this."

But what if you stopped waiting?

> ⋆ **Wake-Up Call**
> No one can give you permission to dream. That power has always belonged to you.

Permission to dream the dream leads to the power to live the dream. When I gave myself permission to fully embrace my dream of parenthood, the power to live that dream was released in me, and the power of that dream was released into the universe. I remember the moment I told my cousin, and later my to-be-husband on our first date, that I wanted to be a parent. The wall came crashing down, and my dream expanded. It became bigger than me, and now it was no longer just mine. There was space, space for others to contribute to the manifestation of the dream and the joy that it would one day bring. By giving myself permission and power to dream, I unknowingly encouraged others to give themselves permission and power to dream, too. And together, we brought that dream to life. Her name is Zelia.

Who Told Us That We Couldn't?

"What do you want to be when you grow up?" We answered boldly, with excitement and certainty. We didn't hesitate to imagine ourselves soaring through space, captivating an audience, or changing the world. We dreamed without limits, played without boundaries, and spoke without doubt.

But somewhere along the way, the dreaming stopped.

Maybe it happened slowly, one comment, one dismissive laugh at a time. Perhaps someone gently teased, "That's cute, but what's your backup plan?" Or maybe someone flat-out told you, "Be realistic. That's never going to happen."

These seemingly small moments shaped our beliefs. They made us question our instincts and convinced us that dreaming big was irresponsible, foolish, or meant only for someone smarter, luckier, richer, or braver. We internalized rules handed down through generations: "Dream smaller. Play safe. Be practical."

Over time, we learned to silence our dreams. We tucked them away, promising we'd revisit them someday. But someday turned into never, and our dreams faded further into the background.

We didn't stop dreaming overnight. It happened gradually, almost unnoticed, as we absorbed rules we never consciously chose to follow. These invisible guidelines shaped our lives, success, and sense of possibility.

Do any of these sound familiar?

I need to be practical.

It's too late for me to start something new.

I should be grateful for what I have.

Dreaming is selfish.

People like me don't get to do things like that.

These messages, repeated enough, feel undeniable. They become boundaries silently guiding every hesitation and quiet settling for less.

But those rules? They weren't written by truth. They were born of fear. Passed down by people who were trying to protect us or protect themselves. And over time, we mistook their caution for clarity.

It's no wonder that dreaming came to feel like a risk.

But maybe... It's time to wonder what else might be possible.

Misconceptions About Dreaming

Our lives have become reflections of someone else's limitations rather than expressions of our courage.

But they don't have to stay this way.

- Dreaming doesn't mean neglecting responsibilities. It means aligning your responsibilities with your authentic self, so you create harmony rather than conflict.

- Dreaming big is not unrealistic. It's bold. Realism sets limits, but boldness opens doors, creates opportunities, and reshapes reality.

- Dreams are not luxuries. They're essential for a thriving, vibrant life. Dreams fuel our growth, purpose, and joy. Without dreams, life loses its spark.

Dreams don't disappear. They're always there, whispering beneath the surface. And the person who silenced your heart cannot hold power over you unless you let them.

No One Can Take Away Your Permission to Dream

I grew up in a home built by dreams, surrounded by dreamers. My grandfather, born in the American South in 1915, was a serial dreamer, seemingly practical and responsible on the outside but passionately adventurous within. As a young man, he played baseball for the Negro Leagues, was a hoofer (tap dancer) with members of the musical group the Ink Spots before they gained fame, and traveled the country on freight trains. Later, he opened a family-run restaurant, traveled the world, bought homes and rental properties, and drove Cadillacs proudly. A new one every five years. When he dreamed of living in Hawaii, he searched for property there; when his dream shifted to Spain, he and my grandmother started learning Spanish in their 60s. My grandmother was his perfect partner. She might have teased him about the impracticality of Spain, but she packed her bags anyway.

My mother carried on this legacy of bold dreaming, traveling alone through Europe, becoming an art museum docent, learning French, and launching her own business after retirement. Not to mention all the dreams she held for me. Dreaming was simply the air we breathed.

But outside of the family, my dreams were challenged and doubted.

I don't remember a specific moment when someone told me, "You can't dream." But I do remember when I stopped. It was around first grade, in 1969. Something shifted. I stopped raising my hand. I stopped offering ideas. I started standing with my back to the wall, quietly watching while other kids played, volunteered, and spoke freely.

I didn't have the words for it then, but I could feel it. As a young Black child, the world around me sent quiet but powerful signals: Don't be too much. Don't be too loud. Don't be too visible. No one said it out loud, but the message was clear.

"This world wasn't made for *your* dreams."

So, I got quiet. I started shrinking. I started believing my dream shouldn't be spoken out loud.

Gradually, I began to hide my dreams, believing that it was necessary for acceptance and safety. I stopped sharing my dreams and watched life pass me by.

But I wasn't happier. I was merely surviving. Eventually, I realized that to be happy, to truly live, I had to reclaim my dreams. Like Dorothy in *The Wizard of Oz*, I discovered I'd had the power within me all along to return home to myself. And so, I did.

> ★ **Wake-Up Call**
> No one else can give you permission to dream. The permission is yours alone to grant.

DREAMER SPOTLIGHT:
DR. MARTIN LUTHER KING JR.
(Civil Rights Activist)
A Dream That Changed the World

My experience taught me that dreaming is transformative. Every dream has the potential to ignite change and reshape history. Dr. Martin Luther King Jr. exemplifies this truth profoundly. He didn't wait for permission. He boldly stood and declared a vision of a world shaped by equality, justice, and unity.

On August 28th, 1963, my father called to tell my mother that he wouldn't be home for dinner. A friend of his, who was a reporter, had invited my father to go with him to a march in Washington, D.C. "And bring your camera." My dad was an amateur photographer. "I'm going to need some pictures to go with my article." The march was only a few hours away from Philadelphia, so my dad jumped in his car and made the trip. This was the March on Washington for Freedom and Jobs, and Dr. Martin Luther King Jr. was one of the speakers. "I have a dream."

In his iconic "I Have a Dream" speech, Dr. King vividly painted a future where freedom and equality were realities for everyone, regardless of race. His dream inspired millions, rallied a nation, and changed the course of history. He defied the skepticism of his time, proving that one person's dream could ignite a movement that reshapes society.

Dr. King's unwavering belief in his dream and his courage to share it openly remind us that dreams are not merely personal. They have the power to resonate, inspire, and mobilize.

Your dream, like Dr. King's, can influence both you and the world around you.

Dream Activation Exercise: Writing Your Own Permission Slip

Take a piece of paper or use the template below, and write:

"I, _____, give myself full permission to dream without limits. I am allowed to want more. I am worthy of the dream that calls to me, and I do not need anyone's approval to pursue it."

Visualization Exercise: Stepping Into Your Dream

Close your eyes. Imagine vividly living your dream. What do you see, hear, and feel? Who is with you? Take time to fully embrace this vision. Remember these emotions; they are your fuel.

Reflection questions:

1. What's a dream you've been hesitant to admit, even to yourself?

2. What's one belief that has held you back from fully embracing your dream?

3. What would it feel like to step into your dream with confidence, knowing you already have permission?

Write down your answers.

Remember that permission slip? Now, it's time to use it.

BONUS: Permission Reinforcement Ritual

Write your permission slip daily. Record and listen to it. Share it publicly or privately in supportive communities. Make reaffirmation a habit.

Final Thoughts: No One is Coming to Save Your Dream

There will never be a perfect moment. No one is going to come along and hand you your dream or tell you it's safe to pursue it.

That's your job.

And the moment you decide to claim it, the moment you stop asking for permission and start owning your dream, is the moment everything changes.

Because your dream matters. And you don't need permission to live it.

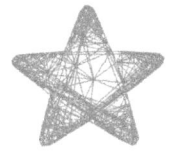

CHAPTER 3

FROM WISHING TO COMMITTING

"Nothing will work unless you do." [4]

—Dr. Maya Angelou

Wishing feels good. It keeps things soft, safe, untouched by the risk of disappointment. Wishing says, *"I hope this happens someday."* Commitment? Commitment shows up in sneakers and sweat. It says, *"I'm willing to do what it takes."*

From Wishes to Dreams: Taking Ownership of Your Vision

Have you ever found yourself wishing for something to happen? Maybe you've thought, "I wish I had more time,"

---

4   Maya Angelou, *Wouldn't Take Nothing for My Journey Now* (New York: Random House, 1993), 4.

or "I wish success would just find me." Wishes are natural; they express our deepest desires. But here's the truth: wishes keep us waiting.

The real magic begins when you turn those wishes into dreams. Why? Because while a wish depends on external forces, a dream empowers you to take action. Dreams are not passive; they are blueprints for what you can create.

Wishes: Hoping for a Handout

Wishes are like messages in a bottle, sent out into the world with no clear path back. You're hoping someone, something, or the universe itself will take notice and do the heavy lifting for you.

The challenge? Waiting for someone else to fulfill your wish often leads to frustration and stagnation. Wishes rarely come true without action, and that's where many dreams fade.

Dreams: I Can Make It Happen

Dreams are different. A dream says, "I can make this happen." It's an inner commitment, a decision to take ownership of your vision. Dreams demand more from you: effort, focus, and resilience. But in return, they offer empowerment, purpose, and, ultimately, transformation.

The moment you shift from "I wish" to "I can," you've stepped into a new realm, one where, rather than hoping for success, you're creating it.

Prayer: Trusting the Process

Then there's prayer. Prayer means aligning your actions with a higher purpose and trusting the process. When paired with action, prayer can be a powerful force that grounds your dreams in faith and intention.

It's not an either-or situation. You can act on your dreams while trusting the universe (or whatever you believe in) to guide you along the way. But remember, faith without action is just a wish.

How to Shift From Wishing to Dreaming

If you're ready to stop wishing and start dreaming, here are three steps to get you started:

1. Own Your Vision
   Be crystal clear on what you want. Define your dream in vivid detail. What does success look like? How will it feel when you get there?

2. Take Bold Action
   Every dream starts with a single step. Break your big vision down into smaller, achievable actions. Focus on progress, not perfection.

3. Stay Connected to Your Why
   Why does this dream matter to you? Keep your purpose front and center to fuel your motivation when challenges arise.

DREAMER SPOTLIGHT:
CINDERELLA, TIANA, AND ALADDIN
(Beloved Disney Characters)
From Wish to Action or Sparking the Leap

Let's be honest, Disney movies aren't just about catchy songs and happily-ever-afters. Beneath the magic wands, talking animals, and musical numbers are some surprisingly sharp lessons about ambition, courage, and owning your worth.

And who better to teach us than Cinderella, Tiana, and Aladdin? Their stories are roadmaps for anyone bold enough to have a dream and brave enough to pursue it.

So, let's break it down. No singing mice required.

Each of these characters made a wish that started them on their path. But wishing alone wasn't enough. Something had to happen that pushed them from dream to action. A turning point at which they decided to go for it, no matter how uncertain or scary it felt.

Cinderella: Reclaim What's Already Yours

Cinderella's dream isn't about snagging a prince or twirling around in a ball gown. It's about reclaiming the life she deserves, one filled with dignity, respect, and the kind of belonging that was taken from her.

The Wish: Cinderella sings her dreams to the stars, wishing for a better life beyond her chores and cruelty.

The Turning Point: The invitation to the royal ball gives her a chance to step back into a world where she's valued. Sure, the fairy godmother waves her wand, but the real magic? That's Cinderella finding the courage to show up like she belongs there, because she does.

The Lesson: Sometimes, chasing your dream means reclaiming something you should've never lost in the first place: your confidence, your voice, or your sense of worth. Help might come in unexpected ways, but believing you deserve more? That's on you.

Tiana: Hustle Matters, But So Does Heart

Tiana's got hustle down to a science. Her dream of opening her restaurant drives her to outwork everyone around her. But here's the catch: relentless ambition can blind you to the beauty of the journey, connection, love, and the simple joy of living.

The Wish: Tiana wishes on the evening star, hoping it will help her fulfill her father's dream of owning a restaurant.

The Turning Point: When her dream feels like it's slipping away after she loses her chance at buying the sugar mill, she realizes success means finding a balance between ambition and connection, between working hard and actually living.

The Lesson: Hustle will get you far, but heart keeps you going. Real success isn't just about what you build, it's about the relationships you nurture along the way.

Aladdin: You Don't Have to Fake It to Make It

Aladdin thinks his only shot at a better life is becoming someone else. So, he dreams of being a prince, believing that status will finally make him worthy of love and success. Spoiler alert: It doesn't.

The Wish: Aladdin rubs the magic lamp and wishes to be a prince so he can win Jasmine's heart and leave his life as a "street rat" behind.

The Turning Point: The magic lamp gives him the power to look the part, but it's not until Aladdin embraces who he really is, flaws, insecurities, and all, that things start to shift. Only then does he finally begin to live his dream, on his own terms.

The Lesson: You don't need to fake it to make it. Owning your authenticity is the most powerful thing you can do. Pretending to be something you're not might open doors, but it won't keep them open.

The Real Magic? It's Already in You

Cinderella didn't wait around for someone to rescue her; she believed she deserved better. Tiana learned that ambition needs room for love and joy. And Aladdin? He discovered that being real is the ultimate power move.

Here's the takeaway:

- Courage helps you claim what's already yours.
- Balance keeps you grounded while you chase those big goals.

- Authenticity turns dreams into something real.

Your version of the ball, the restaurant, or the magic carpet ride might look completely different (unless you've got a genie, in which case, let's talk). But the process? It's the same for all of us.

So, what's your next bold step? Whatever it is, own it. Because the magic? You've had it all along.

Dream Activation Exercise:

JOURNAL PROMPTS

Cinderella – Reclaim What's Already Yours

Prompt:

What part of yourself have you silenced or hidden to survive?

Where in your life have you been waiting for permission?

What would reclaiming your worth look like today?

Tiana – Hustle with Heart

Prompt:

Where has ambition kept you moving but not fully living?

What have you postponed until "someday"?

What relationships, joys, or parts of yourself need more space as you pursue your dream?

Aladdin – You Don't Have to Fake It to Make It

Prompt:

Where have you felt the need to "perform" to be accepted or successful?

What parts of you are you ready to stop hiding?

What would it look like to show up fully as yourself—and trust that it's enough?

DREAM ARCHETYPE QUIZ:
Which Dreamer Are You?

Instructions:

Choose the option that feels most like you. At the end, tally which letter you chose most to discover your dream archetype.

1. What's the biggest obstacle you face with your dream?

A. I'm not sure I deserve it anymore.

B. I'm exhausted from chasing it all alone.

C. I'm afraid I'll be rejected if I show the real me.

2. When things get hard, your default is to:

A. Shrink and keep your head down.

B. Push harder and do more.

C. Put on a mask and pretend everything's fine.

3. What would *actually* feel like success to you?

A. Finally being seen, respected, and valued.

B. Building something meaningful *and* enjoying the journey.

C. Being fully yourself and still being embraced.

4. What kind of support do you most crave?

A. Someone reminding me I'm worthy.

B. Someone reminding me to rest and receive.

C. Someone reminding me I don't have to perform.

5. What's the boldest thing you *haven't* done yet?

A. Reclaim my voice and power.

B. Let others in and trust the process.

C. Show up fully without trying to be perfect.

RESULTS

Mostly A's — You're a Cinderella Dreamer

Your journey is about **reclaiming** what was taken—confidence, worth, joy. Your dream has been quietly waiting for you all along. It's time to rise, no permission slip required.

Mostly B's — You're a Tiana Dreamer

You're a builder and a doer, but don't forget to *be*. Your dream needs heart, not just hustle. Make space for rest, love, and softness. That's where the magic lives.

Mostly C's — You're an Aladdin Dreamer

You've spent too long trying to earn your place by being what others expect. Your real power is in authenticity. Drop the disguise. You're more than enough as you are.

Commitment Clarity Exercise

Prompt:

Write down a dream you've been "wishing" for.

Then answer:

- What have I been waiting for?
- What am I afraid of?
- What would committing to this dream look like—today?

Close with:

"I commit to taking the next bold step toward _____."

Bold Step Tracker

Create a checklist template:

- Named my dream out loud.

- Took one action toward it today.

- Reaffirmed why it matters to me.

- Asked for support.

- Celebrated progress.

Use this as a weekly ritual.

Final Thoughts: You Already Have What You Need

Dreams don't ask for perfection. They ask for presence, for courage, for one small step in the direction of possibility.

You don't need to wait for clarity, confidence, or someone else's approval. The dream is already yours. The permission is already yours. The tools? You'll gather them as you go.

The shift begins now: from hoping to creating, from hiding to becoming.

So, if you've been waiting for a sign... this is it. Let's take that first bold step, together.

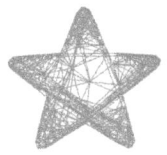

CHAPTER 4

THE COURAGE TO WANT MORE

Have you ever felt guilty for wanting more? Maybe you've thought, *I should just be grateful for what I have.* Or maybe you've told yourself that dreaming bigger is selfish, that other people have real problems, and you should be happy with where you are.

> ★ **Wake-Up Call**
> Wanting more isn't greedy; it's growth.

You were never meant to stay exactly the same, to shrink into something small and comfortable. The desire to grow, to expand, to create. That's what makes you alive.

In fact, studies show that over 60% of people report feeling unfulfilled in their current lives, even if everything *looks* good on the outside. So, if you've ever felt this way, you're not alone.

Why is wanting more so hard to claim?

The Guilt of Wanting More

I had finally checked all the boxes. A successful year. A home. Two dogs. A husband I adored. A school we loved for our daughter. A job in real estate that paid well, respected my time, and let me be present for my family.

By every measure, I was thriving. I had what so many people strive for. I was doing what I was supposed to do. And I was deeply, truly grateful.

But under the surface, beneath the rhythm of school drop-offs and weekend open houses, there was something I couldn't name. At first, it felt like restlessness. Then maybe boredom. But eventually, I had to admit: It was longing.

I wanted something more. Not more stuff. Not more status. *More purpose. More depth. More alignment.*

I had always wanted to help people build something real. Not just homes, but futures. Particularly parents. To walk alongside exceptional parents raising extraordinary kids. To help them feel less alone, more grounded, surer of their path. To empower them. To see their family thrive. And to be there during the moments when they needed an ear to listen, a shoulder to cry on, or a heart to connect and celebrate with.

And as soon as I let that truth rise to the surface, *the guilt followed.*

How dare I want more when I already had so much? What kind of person risks stability, risks gratitude, risks *good enough*? How selfish must I be to even consider walking away from a life so many would love to have?

That inner war was quiet but relentless. I didn't talk about it at first. I smiled. I stayed productive. I kept moving. But the ache stayed with me through closings, through celebrations, even through laughter.

It wasn't dissatisfaction, but *truth*. And truth doesn't let go once it finds its voice.

So, one day, I walked into my manager's office. And I told her, "I'm leaving to start my own coaching business." Just like that, I declared what I wanted. I chose it. I stepped forward.

The guilt didn't disappear. But something softer rose alongside it. Not certainty. Not pride.

Permission. Permission from myself to want more.

And with it, I finally exhaled. Because wanting more doesn't make you selfish.

It makes you honest. It makes you alive. It means you're still listening.

Why Dreaming Can Feel Selfish

Maybe the notion came from family, where success was measured by stability, and taking risks felt irresponsible. Or from society, where some are told they deserve success while others are expected to settle. Or perhaps it came from past failures, where wanting more only led to disappointment. Somehow, we learned that wanting more was wrong. That it meant we were ungrateful or too ambitious or asking for too much.

For many women and people of color, there's an added cultural narrative, one that says, "Don't take up too much space." Wanting more can feel like defying centuries of conditioning that taught us to be content with less. When we pursue "more," we can be met with greater scrutiny than our counterparts, every mistake magnified, and our ambition is framed as arrogance, our desire as greed. The unspoken lesson? Wanting more makes us difficult, ungrateful, and selfish. We are better off staying in our place, smiling politely, and being content with what we have.

This is why it is no surprise that many of us, instead of owning our desires, downplay them. We tell ourselves:

I shouldn't ask for more.

I should just be happy where I am.

Who am I to want something bigger?

But what if we flipped the question?

Instead of asking, *Who am I to dream big?* What if we asked, *Who am I not to?*

The Shift from "Who Am I?" to "Why Not Me?"

The people who achieve big things, the artists, the innovators, the leaders, aren't necessarily the smartest, the wealthiest, or the most talented. They're the ones who decided to want more and stopped apologizing for it.

Let's flip some of the most common inner scripts:

- *Who am I to start my own business?* Who am I **not** to bring my vision to life?

- *Who am I to speak on that stage?* Who better than me to share that message?

- *Who am I to ask for more money?* Why shouldn't my value be fully recognized?

★ **Wake-Up Call**
You are the only person who can stand for your dream.

DREAMER SPOTLIGHT: CYNTHIA ERIVO
(Singer, Actress)
Owning the Dream

. . . .

Before *Wicked*, before Elphaba, Cynthia Erivo was just a girl growing up in London, the daughter of Nigerian immigrants. Raised in a working-class neighborhood, she developed a love for music and performance early on. She trained at the Royal Academy of Dramatic Art and took roles in theater and television, honing her craft away from the global spotlight. Hers was a path full of rejection, diligence, and doubt, but her commitment to her dream never wavered.

She didn't follow the "safe" path. She could have played small. She could have listened to the doubts, the voices saying her chosen path was too hard or too competitive. But she didn't.

She stepped into spaces where people like her weren't always welcomed and made them hers. She chose roles that mattered. She took creative risks. She built a career that was impactful.

One of the most impactful performances I have ever seen was Cynthia Erivo's Broadway debut in *The Color Purple*. At the time, she was unknown in the U.S. outside of theater circles, but there was already buzz about the stir this young artist was creating in London. Experiencing her doing what she loved without holding back was witnessing a star being born. Her performance of "I'm Here" in the second act was *the* moment. For her, it was a triumph; for us, the audience, it was a whisper that said: *watch her, go with her, experience and be inspired by her*. She had the dream, and now she had the community and support to live it fully, and on her terms.

And she has continued to soar. With her portrayal of Elphaba in the long-awaited film adaptation of *Wicked*, Cynthia stepped into an iconic role, and redefined it. Her voice, her presence, her power lit up the screen and reminded us of what's possible when a dream is lived without apology. Her dream inspired others. It gave people a voice.

> ★ **Wake-Up Call**
> Dreaming isn't just about what you get; it's about what you give.

"Everyone deserves the chance to fly." [5]

—Elphaba, *Wicked*

Dream Activation Exercise:

Practical Steps to Embrace Your Dream

1. **Acknowledge Your Desire**: Stop downplaying what you want. Say it out loud or write it down.

---

5   Stephen Schwartz and Winnie Holzman, *Wicked* (Broadway Musical, 2003).

2. **Challenge the Guilt**: Recognize that feeling guilty doesn't mean your desire is wrong. Examine where the guilt comes from.

3. **Seek Inspiration**: Surround yourself with stories of dreamers who made it despite the odds.

4. **Take One Bold Step**: Whether it's sharing your vision with someone or starting a new project, make a move today.

5. **Visualize Success**: Picture yourself living your dream, and let that feeling motivate you.

Five-Day Dream Challenge (Bonus)

Day 1: Name your dream. Be bold.

Day 2: Identify what's held you back.

Day 3: Reframe the guilt.

Day 4: Visualize the moment your dream comes true.

Day 5: Share your dream with someone you trust.

Visualization Exercise: Step into Your Dream

Close your eyes and imagine your dream as if it's already real. See yourself living it. What are you doing? Who is with you? How does it feel to know that you've claimed this vision? Hold on to that feeling; it's yours to keep.

Dream Activation Exercise: Defining Your Boldest Ambition

It's easy to downplay our dreams. To make them smaller, safer.

But not today.

Take out a journal, a notebook, or open a blank page and answer these questions honestly:

- If fear didn't exist, what would you want most?

- What's a dream that excites you but also scares you?

- What's the boldest, most audacious version of your dream?

- What would your life look like if you trusted yourself fully?

Write it down. Own it.

And then remind yourself: You're allowed to want more.

Reflective Journaling Prompts

- When have I felt guilty for wanting more?

- What messages did I grow up with about ambition?

- Where in my life am I playing small?

- Who inspires me to dream bigger?

Letter from Your Future Self

Write a letter from your future self, the version of you who claimed your dream. What do they say? What did they overcome? What do they know now that you've forgotten?

Let that voice be your guide.

Dreams Don't Leave You

> *"Ideas are driven by a single impulse: to be made manifest... [The idea] will try to get your attention... but when it finally realizes that you're oblivious to its message, it will move on to someone else."* [6]

—Elizabeth Gilbert, *Big Magic*

And it's true, ideas can be fleeting. They'll leave if you don't act. But dreams are different.

Dreams live inside you. They're part of your being. Even when buried or ignored, a dream lingers, quietly waiting for the moment you're ready.

You carry it, sometimes without even knowing. And when you're finally ready to listen, it will still be there. Yours. Always.

Final Thoughts: Give Yourself Permission to Want More

Dreaming big is necessary, not selfish.

---

[6] Elizabeth Gilbert, Big Magic: Creative Living Beyond Fear (New York: Riverhead Books, 2015), 34-35.

Every time you step into your dream, you create space for others to do the same.

Don't shrink. Don't apologize. Step forward.

The world doesn't need smaller dreams. It needs yours.

"Messy isn't a mistake. It's just the dream doing squats."

—Kiran

SECTION TWO

THE MAGIC IS IN THE MESS

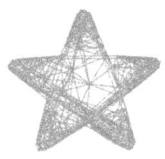

CHAPTER 5

FROM DREAMING TO DOING

Dreaming is easy. Doing is where most people get stuck.

You've given yourself permission. You've embraced the idea that you deserve to dream big. But now comes the part that separates wishful thinking from actual transformation, from taking the first step.

> ★ **Wake-Up Call**
> The gap between wanting and doing is where many dreams are left waiting.

So, how do you cross that gap?
One step at a time.

Crossing the Gap: The Dream Bridge

Think of your journey like a bridge from where you are now to where your dream lives. There are four planks:

Decide – Say yes to your dream. Even if it scares you. Even if you don't have it all figured out yet.

Act – Take one step forward, no matter how small. Action is commitment made visible.

Reflect – Pause to learn. What worked? What didn't? What do you need next?

Repeat – Go again. Keep going. Momentum is built through consistency.

This bridge doesn't require a map. It just needs movement. When you walk it daily, even briefly, it becomes a part of your identity.

Turning Dreams Into Decisions

A dream without action is just a fantasy.

Maybe you've been waiting for the right moment, the perfect conditions, or some kind of cosmic sign that it's time to start.

> ★ **Wake-Up Call**
> There is no perfect moment. The only way forward is to decide.

And decisions happen through action. Real-world, visible, measurable action.

Right now, think about your dream. The big, bold, beautiful thing you want. Got it? Good. Now ask yourself:

What's one tiny step I can take today? What action, no matter how small, will move me forward?

Waiting is a habit. And so is taking action. One leads to inertia. The other leads to progress.

Which are you choosing?

Taking Action

Let's start simple and small. Instead of mapping the whole journey, choose the very first step you can take this week. Momentum starts small.

Here are five possible simple steps to choose from:

1. **Clear a Corner** – Choose a small physical space (a desk, drawer, or shelf) to dedicate to your dream. Clearing it signals you're making room for what's next.

2. **Gather Supplies** – Pick up a fresh notebook, open a new document, or grab a folder. Give your dream a tangible "home" to live in.

3. **Create a Reminder** – Find a word or image that represents your dream and set it as your phone background or post it on a sticky note. Let it quietly remind you each day.

4. **Mark the Start** – Plan a date to officially "begin" and put it on your calendar. Even if it's small, that day becomes a milestone you'll look back on.

5. **Find Your Fuel** – Build a short playlist,
    light a candle, or create a simple ritual that
    puts you in the right headspace. It doesn't
    have to be elaborate, just something that
    says, *I'm showing up for my dream.*

Every big dream begins with one small choice. Make yours today and trust that momentum will follow.

The Dreamer's Obstacle Course

We all face hurdles. You're not alone. Here are a few common obstacles and how to reframe them:

Obstacle: "I don't know where to start."

Reframe: "Start anywhere. Clarity comes from doing. Every first step reveals the next."

Obstacle: "It has to be perfect."

Reframe: "Done is better than perfect. Perfectionism is fear in disguise."

Obstacle: "What if I fail?"

Reframe: "What if you learn something that leads to your breakthrough? Every setback is an opportunity for growth."

Obstacle: "I'm too late."

Reframe: "Now is always the right time to begin. The best time was then. The next best time is now."

Use this obstacle course not to avoid the hurdles, but to learn how to leap over them.

The Power of Imperfect Action

People love to talk about motivation, as if it's the spark that gets everything going. But here's the real secret to making dreams happen:

> ★ **Wake-Up Call**
> Action comes first. Motivation follows.

Most of us wait for a feeling. We wait to feel inspired, confident, clear. But more often than not, that feeling never arrives. Because readiness isn't a prerequisite but a *result*. Readiness comes from movement. Clarity comes from doing. Confidence comes from keeping your promise to yourself, one imperfect action at a time.

You don't need a fully formed plan. You don't need to have it all figured out. You just need the courage to take the first step, even if it's messy, awkward, or slightly terrifying. That one small step creates motion. And motion builds momentum.

Imperfect action is powerful because it interrupts the loop of hesitation. It's the difference between dreaming about the life you want and *building* it. Think of your dream as a foggy road at night. Your headlights only show a few feet ahead, but you can drive across the entire country that way. One turn of the wheel at a time.

So, stop waiting to feel ready. Push. Stumble. Step. Your next move will reveal the next, and the next after that. And before you know it, you're moving. And movement is what makes dreams real.

DREAMER SPOTLIGHT: LIN-MANUEL MIRANDA
(Composer, Playwright, Actor)
The Urgency of Now

. . . .

Lin-Manuel Miranda wasn't waiting for his turn; he was writing it.

He was a theater kid with hip-hop in his headphones and salsa in his soul. His world was full of rhythm, rhyme, and culture, but the stages he loved didn't reflect it. He could recite Sondheim and Biggie Smalls in the same breath, and yet he rarely saw anyone like himself at the center of the stories he loved most.

But instead of shrinking, he scribbled. He wrote in notebooks, on napkins, in margins. Music, poetry, characters that sounded like home. While others partied in college, Miranda was writing full musicals. He didn't know how his dream would happen, just that it had to.

Because for him, the dream was the very oxygen he breathed.

When he started writing *In the Heights*, Miranda was chasing belonging. He poured his whole self into the script: the Spanglish, the corner bodegas, the joy, and the heartbreak of a neighborhood in transition. It was messy, musical, and unapologetically Latino.

It took years. Dozens of rewrites. Critics who didn't get it. Funders who passed. Friends who asked, "Why this story?" But Miranda couldn't let it go. The stories of his people, their accents, their dreams, their heartbreaks, had been left out of the American theater canon for too long. And he wanted to reclaim space.

When *In the Heights* hit Broadway, it electrified. It turned theater on its head. Suddenly, salsa met stage lights, and audiences saw Washington Heights in harmony, heartbreak, and hope.

Then came the whisper of the next idea. *Hamilton.* A hip-hop retelling of the story of America's founding fathers. He envisioned it as a mixtape rather than a musical. The world thought he was out of his mind. But he wasn't writing to impress the world. He was writing to awaken it.

When *Hamilton* opened, it broke records *and exceeded* expectations. The founding story of America was being told by Black and Brown voices, and a Puerto Rican kid from upper Manhattan was the face of American history, remixed.

Miranda had done something rare; he'd created art that was critically acclaimed, commercially successful, and culturally seismic. But here's what makes Miranda's story different.

He never stopped hustling. He never stopped giving. He never stopped lifting the mic to someone else's mouth and saying, *Your voice matters, too.* He used his voice to raise funds for Puerto Rico. To create platforms for young writers. To collaborate with Disney, Pixar, and stage companies around the globe, always with one foot in the community.

He reminds us that the dream doesn't end when it's realized. It evolves. It expands. It calls on you to ask, "Now that I've made it in, how do I hold the door open for others?"

Lin-Manuel Miranda chased truth. And in doing so, he turned his voice into a movement and his dream into a megaphone.

Dream Activation Exercise: Taking Your First Step Today

It's time to close the gap between dreaming and doing.

Grab a notebook, your phone, or any writing device you have on hand, and answer this:

What's ONE small step I can take toward my dream TODAY?

How can I act before I feel ready?

What's something I can do in the next ten minutes that moves me forward?

Then revisit your answer tomorrow:

- Did I do it?
- What worked?
- What got in the way?
- What's my next step?

Track your progress. Celebrate small wins. Keep going. Every day is a new chance to say yes again.

BONUS: Seven-Day Momentum-Builder Challenge

Commit to five minutes of action per day. Set a timer. Choose one tiny task. Do it. Track your streak and build your doing muscle. At the end of seven days, reflect on how far you've come.

Final Thoughts: Start Small, But Start

Don't worry about huge leaps. Focus on taking consistent steps.

Every small step adds up. Every imperfect action builds momentum.

So, stop waiting. Stop planning. Stop doubting.

Just start.

Your dream isn't waiting for the perfect moment.

It's waiting for you.

You don't have to leap.

You only need to lean forward.

The dream moves with you.

CHAPTER 6

OBSTACLES, ROADBLOCKS, AND THE MESSY MIDDLE

At the beginning of any dream, everything feels exciting. You have big ideas, a powerful vision, and that initial rush of momentum that fuels your early steps. And then, reality hits.

Suddenly, things don't go as planned. Emails go unanswered. Money gets tight. Doubt creeps in like a shadow. You start wondering: Was this a mistake? Am I even cut out for this?

Welcome to the messy middle. The part where most people quit. The part that tests your faith, your stamina, your why. But not you. You're still here.

Before You Go On...

Close your eyes for a moment and breathe. Think about a time you wanted to give up.

What did it feel like in your body? What did your inner voice say?

Now, imagine what it would've felt like to move through it, anyway. You're still here. That means something.

Handling Setbacks Without Losing Momentum

"If you take Resistance at its word, you deserve everything you get. Resistance is always lying and always full of shit." [7]

—Steven Pressfield

Every dreamer faces obstacles. That's confirmation that you're on a path worth pursuing. The question isn't if challenges will come. They will. The real question is: How will you respond?

Setbacks don't mean your dream is impossible. They're proof that you're in motion. And anything in motion will face resistance. Think of setbacks like growing pains, uncomfortable but essential.

Here's how to keep moving forward:

Expect obstacles. Don't be surprised when they show up. Make them part of your plan.

Separate setbacks from self-worth. Failing doesn't mean you are a failure. It means you're learning.

Adjust, don't abandon. Detours don't mean dead ends. Revise your strategy. Keep the dream. Talk back to doubt. That inner critic is loudest in the middle part of your journey. Answer it with truth, not fear. Most importantly:

---

7 Steven Pressfield, *The War of Art: Break Through the Blocks and Win Your Inner Creative Battles* (Black Irish Entertainment, 2002), 8.

Don't pause your dream just because things aren't going perfectly. Progress is still progress, even when it's messy.

Even this book is an example. When I first committed to writing it, I told myself I'd finish in three months. In reality, it took closer to nine. Along the way, life threw me plenty of reasons to quit—the passing of my mother, interruptions from travel, scheduling conflicts, and even my own self-doubt whispering that maybe I wasn't the one to write this. Any one of those could have stopped me. And yet, in the middle of those challenges, life also gave me a gift: a new name. That name was a turning point. It reshaped how I saw myself and became part of the story this book needed to tell. Instead of abandoning the dream, I chose to take the pivots, embrace the detours, and keep going. And in the process, the book survived the bumps and even grew because of them. Each twist, each loss, and each shift in identity added depth and truth I couldn't have written without living it.

The Nature of the Messy Middle

These strategies will help, but they don't eliminate the discomfort of the journey. Let's name what it really feels like to be stuck in the middle.

What makes the messy middle so hard is that it feels endless. You're far from the start, but not yet near the finish. You've used up your early excitement, but you haven't seen the payoff yet.

This middle space is a crucible. It refines you. It asks: Do you really want this? Will you keep showing up even when it's uncomfortable? Can you trust yourself enough to continue?

Endurance is a skill. And like all skills, it strengthens with practice. The more you stay with the process, the more resilient you become.

You're not alone in this space.

Between Caterpillar and Butterfly

This isn't the before or the after.

This is the in-between.

The place where time slows and the outside world fades.

The past can't pull you back.

The future hasn't taken shape.

Here in the cocoon, nothing moves, and yet, everything is changing.

The goo, the mess.

Breaking down while building up.

It's the sacred stillness where clarity whispers,

where wounds begin to close,

where the dream starts to feel real.

This is a pause that can't be rushed.

Settle in.

There is a butterfly waiting on the other side.

DREAMER SPOTLIGHT: DAN LEVY
(Actor, Writer, Producer)
From Rejection to Revolution

> ⭐ **Wake-Up Call**
> Every dream that matters passes through this middle space. It's where your commitment is tested. It's where you either pause, pivot, or push forward.

And it's also where breakthroughs are quietly born.

One of the clearest examples doesn't come from an overnight rags-to-riches story, but from someone who spent years stuck in the middle, unsure if anyone would ever care about the vision he believed in so deeply.

Television writer and producer Dan Levy wasn't sure he fit. Growing up in a famous family—his father is actor and comedian Eugene Levy—Dan often felt more awkward than accomplished, more anxious than ambitious. He wrestled with panic attacks and deep insecurity, especially around being openly gay in an industry that still whispered its acceptance rather than declared it. While others seemed to move forward with ease, Dan kept quiet, unsure how to build a dream when he couldn't yet see where he belonged.

There's a particular kind of pain in knowing you have something to offer but not seeing a space for it. He tried hosting, writing, and acting, but nothing stuck. He was always on the edge of something, but never quite inside. He kept hearing versions of: "You're too niche. Too specific. Too different."

Have you ever felt like the world only wants the safe version of you? Dan did. And for a while, he started to believe it. Then one day, he stopped waiting to be invited in and started building something of his own.

The birth of the television show *Schitt's Creek* was messy. Dan co-created the show with his father, but even then, the doubts followed. The show premiered quietly in Canada. U.S. networks weren't interested. Critics didn't immediately praise it. And for years, the audience was small.

Behind the scenes, Dan wore every hat: writer, showrunner, actor, producer. He poured himself into the work, not just to prove others wrong, but to prove to himself that the dream was real. That it mattered.

The pressure took a toll. He often worked sixteen-hour days and once admitted he nearly quit after Season 2 due to burnout and fear. He worried the show would never be "enough." That he wasn't enough.

He shared in interviews how imposter syndrome gnawed at him: What if I'm not the kind of person who gets to succeed like this? What if my best just isn't sufficient? What if I'm wasting everyone's time? But he persevered, even in fear. He kept writing. Kept creating. Kept holding space for something tender and hopeful. The show became a place where queer love wasn't tragic, where people changed for the better, and where family could grow in unexpected ways.

Every season, Dan and his team told the kind of story they wished had existed when they were younger. And slowly, the world began to notice.

Schitt's Creek didn't explode; it simmered.

It built its audience person by person, moment by moment, until one day, it grew from a hidden gem to a phenomenon. The final season swept the Emmys, breaking records and making history. Dan became a symbol of perseverance.

But the dream didn't end with applause.

Dan used his platform to support LGBTQ+ advocacy, create more inclusive spaces in fashion and entertainment, and launch new projects centered on authenticity. He proved that the dream is never just about you; it's about what your courage makes possible for others. He turned anxiety into bold art. Fear into connection. Uncertainty into a universal truth. We don't just need stories of success. We also need stories of near-failures. That shows us what it looks like to keep going when no one's watching.

> ★ **Wake-Up Call**
> The messy middle is where we build the strength to finish.

Dan Levy's dream bloomed because he stayed the course.

Dream Activation Exercise: Overcoming Obstacles with Strategy

You're facing something hard. That's okay. Let's move through it together.

Grab your journal or notes app and answer these questions:

What's the real problem? (Is it fear? Is it a resource issue? A confidence dip? Identify the root.)

What's one way I can move through it? (Can you try a smaller version of your plan? Can you reframe the story you're telling yourself?)

Who can I ask for support? (A mentor? A peer? A community? You don't have to go it alone.)

Now, take one action based on what you uncovered. Just one. Action turns pressure into power.

Final Thoughts: The Messy Middle is Where Growth Happens

The difference between dreamers and doers? Doers don't quit. They cry. They pause. They rage. They rest. They get back up.

So, when it gets hard, and it will, don't give up. Give it time. Give it grace. Give it another try.

Your dream is waiting on the other side of the obstacle. When you reach it, you'll realize:

You *became* the person who could live that dream.

The road gets messy. Keep going anyway. That's where your power is forged.

Say this aloud:

I am not lost. I am learning. I am not broken. I am becoming. I am not done. I am dreaming forward.

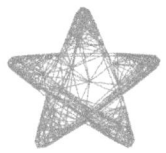

CHAPTER 7

THE DREAMER'S COMMUNITY – FINDING YOUR PEOPLE

Before strategy, before structure, you need support. Every dream begins with a whisper inside one person. But no dream reaches its full potential without others. The people around you, the ones who believe in you, challenge you, hold space for your doubt, and fuel your hope—are essential.

This chapter isn't about community in a general sense. It's about your *dream community*, those rare and radiant souls who see you not just for who you are, but for who you're becoming. The ones who make the journey possible and powerful.

If you've ever felt like you were carrying your dream alone, this chapter is for you.

Let's begin where so many of us do, with the quiet ache of going it alone, and discover how to build the circle that lets your dream breathe, grow, and take flight.

The Loneliness of Dreaming Alone

I believed I had to do it all on my own. The dream of becoming a parent was alive, but it felt fragile, too precious to expose to the world. Sharing it felt risky, and trusting others with it? Even riskier.

But dreams aren't meant to be built alone.

We all hit a point where the weight of doing it alone becomes too much. That moment of quiet longing, a hope not just for your dream to come true, but for someone to believe in it with you. That moment is the start of finding your people.

The Echo Chamber or The First Yes

This isn't about asking for permission. You've already given yourself that. This is about finding someone who will echo your yes, loudly, clearly, and without question. That's what the first yes is. It's resonance.

When the name *Kiran* came to me, my decision to say yes came quickly. No second guessing. I didn't need weeks to weigh it or sit with it. I knew it was mine. Undeniably.

What I needed next was someone to witness it. To meet my yes with their own. To reflect it back—with love.

That person was my daughter, Zelia. She was my **Echo**: the one I trusted to hold the dream with gentle hands and offer it back with grace.

I sent her a text:

"I think I'm changing my name to Kiran."

Her response was instant. A big thumbs-up emoji, simple, joyful, full of love. I felt it in my heart.

My Echo didn't explain the decision or question it. They just said, *"Yes. I see you. I'm with you."*

Your Echo is the person who reminds you that you don't need permission. They won't always be the same person. But you'll know who they are when the moment comes.

Chances are, they're already waiting in the wings, ready to love you forward.

The Right People Elevate Your Dream

Your environment matters. Your circle matters even more. Surround yourself with people who:

- Encourage your vision (not those who make you shrink).
- Challenge you to grow.
- Believe in what's possible.

But how do you find them? And how do you know when you have?

Let's explore.

The Stages of Dream Community

Finding your dream community is a journey.

1. The Search
   You start with longing for understanding,

encouragement, and connection. You may not even know exactly what you need, only that you feel its absence.

2. The Signals
It might be a single supportive message from a friend. Or a stranger's comment that makes you feel seen. These moments are like stars in the night, small signs that you're not alone.

3. The Spark
Then, you meet someone who just gets it. You find collaborators, coaches, fellow dreamers who speak your language. Energy starts to build.

4. The Synergy
Together, you start creating. Celebrating wins. Facing challenges. Your vision feels more real because it's held by someone other than just you.

An Empty Pot and a Dream

At first, your dream might look like an empty pot and a stone. A bold idea. A spark of something real. But not nearly enough. Still, you light the fire. You name the dream. You begin with whatever you have. It's like the classic folktale *Stone Soup*: a traveler starts with just water and a stone, then prompts villagers to each contribute something, onion, carrot, potato, until the pot overflows with a feast far richer than anything they could have made alone.

People might look on with curiosity. Maybe even doubt. But if the dream is true, if the vision is clear, others begin to gather. Someone brings encouragement. Another offers time, a skill, a connection. And just like the villagers adding their ingredient, each small contribution says, "*I believe in this. I want in.*"

That's what building a dream together looks like. Not waiting for perfect alignment.

Not carrying it all alone. But letting others add what they have and watching something greater emerge. Because the first person who joins brings confirmation. And the next one brings momentum. And before you know it, the thing you thought you weren't able to do alone... becomes something you'd never want to do alone again.

That's the real feast. A recipe made of belief, shared effort, and collective heart. And it all starts with one bold invitation: "*I'm making something. Want to help?*"

DREAMER SPOTLIGHT: DREW BARRYMORE

(Actress, Producer, Talk Show Host)
The Power of Being Held

. . . .

Drew Barrymore grew up on movie sets and in headlines. She was seven years old when E.T. made her a household name. Nine, when she picked up smoking. Thirteen when she entered rehab. Fourteen when she was legally emancipated from her parents.

She was famous but not protected. Loved by the public but often left alone in real life.

So she learned to survive. To hustle. To entertain. To smile even when her world was unraveling. But survival isn't the same as connection.

And for a long time, Drew was alone. She spent her twenties trying to rewrite that narrative. She started her own production company. Starred in beloved films. Launched a beauty brand. Got married. Got divorced. Got married again. Got divorced again.

Through it all, she was still smiling. Still shining. Still saying, I'm okay. But inside, she was craving something deeper. Belonging. Softness. Real community.

Then came her daughters. And then… her talk show. That represented a return to herself. Because what she wanted, maybe what she'd always wanted, was to sit in a circle of women, of people, and say, *You're not alone. Me neither.*

The Drew Barrymore Show became more than a stage. It became a space. A kitchen table. A couch. A sanctuary for honest conversations, ugly cries, joyful dances, and soft, slow healing. She showed up as a human being. And people showed up right back.

Today, Drew Barrymore is living a different kind of dream. One where she's whole, surrounded by people who love her, not because she performs, but because she's finally real.

She builds community on-screen and off. She tells the truth. She lifts others. She laughs big and cries hard and reminds us that you don't have to have it all together to be worthy of love.

She was to return not to fame but to herself and find her people along the way. Drew's story reminds us that. Sometimes, the dream looks like a deep breath. A kitchen full of laughter. A friend who says, "You don't have to do this alone."

She teaches us that healing is communal. That joy is magnetic. That you can rebuild your life with the same hands that once held your heartbreak.

And maybe most powerfully, she shows us that the right people don't just see you.

They hold you while you remember who you are.

The Dream Network: Roles That Matter

Not everyone plays the same role in your dream journey. Here are a few essential archetypes to look for:

The Echo – Gives you your first yes.

The Mirror – Reflects your brilliance when you forget it.

The Challenger – Pushes you to grow when you'd rather stay comfortable.

The Connector – Introduces you to people and opportunities you never imagined.

The Anchor – Holds you steady when life gets turbulent.

Where to Look for Your Dream Network

Begin close to home. Your dream network is revealed over time.

Think of the people who make you feel most alive, most yourself. Who listens without fixing? Who celebrates your vision even before it's fully formed? These are clues. Your dream network might include an old teacher, a fellow creative, a quiet encourager, or someone you've yet to meet but already feel drawn to.

Look in places where big questions are welcome: intimate gatherings, purpose-driven communities, storytelling circles, or even the comment section of a post that moved you. You're not just looking for expertise; you're listening for resonance. For those who don't just ask "what do you do?" but "what do you dream?"

The Break

There are plenty of people who won't support us in our dreams from the start, and there are those who become threatened when we grow.

There was a friend who had been in my life for years. They were there for the early steps, when the dream was still fragile, still forming. They encouraged me. Believed in me. But as my dream became clearer, more grounded, and started asking more of me—more time, more visibility, more vulnerability—something between us shifted.

I'd share a win, and they'd change the subject. I'd talk about something I was excited to build, and they'd meet it with silence or a dismissive smile. It didn't feel like curiosity anymore. It felt like discomfort.

At first, I rationalized it. Maybe they didn't get it. Maybe I was imagining things. But deep down, I knew. I was growing, and they didn't know what to do with that.

There wasn't a big blow-up. No confrontation. Just a quiet knowing: *This version of me doesn't fit in that version of us anymore.*

So, I stopped explaining. Stopped shrinking. Stopped chasing the version of our friendship that once was. I didn't stop caring. I just stopped pretending. And without resentment or bitterness, I let the connection drift. Because I couldn't keep holding on to something that no longer held me too. And I couldn't let someone's discomfort become a reason to dim the very thing I'd worked so hard to ignite.

Some people walk with you only so far. And when you realize that, you reach a turning point. A quiet kind of freedom. A freedom that created room for everything that came next. You find new partners, a deeper truth, and a dream that no longer needs to apologize for how brightly it burns.

Who sees not just who you are, but who you're becoming? And what space might open if you stop shrinking to stay connected?

Dream Activation Exercise: Building Your Dream Network

Take a few moments to reflect and journal:

1. **Inventory**: Who currently supports your dream? Who drains your energy?

2. **Vision**: If your dream came true tomorrow, who would you want celebrating with you?

3. **Gap Analysis**: What roles are missing in your community?

4. **Action Plan**: How can you begin connecting with people who elevate your dream?

(Pro tip: Be that person for someone else, too.)

Final Thoughts: You Don't Have to Do This Alone

The right people won't just cheer for your dream; they'll help you shape it, strengthen it, and see it through.

You reading this now means you're already stepping into a wider circle of dreamers. You don't have to have it all figured out. You just have to stay open and keep reaching.

Find them. Dream with them. Build with them.

You were never meant to do this alone.

"The dream isn't a goal. It's who you're becoming."

—Kiran

SECTION THREE

LIVING THE DREAM

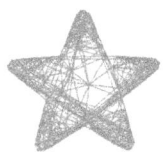

CHAPTER 8

BOLD DREAMS, BOLD ACTION

It's one thing to imagine the possibility: what your life, your work, your impact could become. It's another to say, *I'm doing this*. To risk being seen. To move forward before you feel ready.

Maybe you're standing at that edge right now. Your dream is clear enough to feel but still fragile enough to doubt.

This chapter is for that moment. Because the shift happens not in the vision but in the decision.

Do the Thing. Build the Dream.

My mother told me more than once that I should write a book. She never said what it should be about, just that I should write one, as if she could see something in me that I hadn't fully claimed for myself.

For years, I carried the idea. Mostly in fragments, Facebook posts, blogs, and emails. Workshop scripts that could have been chapters. Reflections that never made it out of my journal. But I didn't start.

I told myself I didn't have time. But the truth was, I didn't have the courage.

Writing this book meant choosing myself in a way I never had. It meant owning what I believe, not just privately, but publicly. It meant saying, *My voice matters. My dream matters.* That's a bold dream: to be seen.

And on January 15, 2025, I finally said yes. I set a bold goal: have the book ready for presale in seventy-five days. I didn't overthink it. I didn't ask for permission. I just began.

I carved out writing time before sunrise. I said no to things I would have once said yes to because this mattered more. I let go of the need to sound impressive and chose to sound real. And word by word, page by page, the dream took form.

I told my mother what I was doing. My Echo. She smiled. She didn't ask for details. She didn't need them. She just said, "Good."

Sixteen days later, she died.

She never got to hold the finished book. But she got to witness me carry out the boldest action of all: I finally started.

And that's what bold action is. It's not perfection. (I didn't finish in seventy-five days.) It's movement. It's declaring, *This is the dream. I'm doing it anyway.*

Because bold dreams don't bloom in someday. They grow in the moments we say yes. Even while we're afraid. They're written. Spoken. Lived.

This chapter is about that moment. The one where you stop circling your dream and start building it. The one where you stop shrinking and start moving. The one where you go all-in.

Because saying yes to a bold dream is a practice. A mindset. A way of showing up fully.

DREAMER SPOTLIGHT: SERENA WILLIAMS
(Tennis Champion, Entrepreneur, Icon)
**Discipline. Persistence.
Stepping Fully Into Greatness.**

. . . .

Serena Williams was born in Compton, California, where opportunities were few, but dreams were big. She and her sister Venus practiced on cracked public courts with borrowed tennis balls. Their father, Richard, had no formal training but a radical vision. He saw champions in his daughters long before the world did.

In those early days, Serena was often underestimated. Her power, her presence, and her personality were too much, too different. But even as a child, Serena held something powerful: belief. The kind that blooms in soil laced with resistance. She was preparing for greatness.

Serena didn't casually dream her way to the top. She worked. She studied the game. She trained when others rested. She faced devastating losses, injuries, and critics who questioned everything about her.

So, she recalibrated.

She evolved from a raw, determined young player into one of the most dominant forces in sports history, male or female. Her presence changed the way people viewed tennis. Her body, her power, her unapologetic confidence? Revolutionary.

She played for everyone who never saw themselves on that court before.

Serena *rewrote* what the dream could look like.

And she didn't stop there.

Serena used her platform to become a businesswoman, investor, fashion designer, and advocate for maternal health and racial equity. She became a mother, and with that, a whole new chapter of purpose began.

She shifted from winning titles to shaping legacies. She expanded beyond tennis without ever leaving the spirit of her dream behind. Because true dreamers change narratives.

Serena reminds us that the boldest dream isn't the one you accomplish. It's the one that keeps growing even after the trophy.

Create Your Dream Ritual

A Joyful Practice to Sustain Your Bold Becoming

You need more than a plan. Develop a ritual, a rhythm that aligns your energy with your dream.

A dream ritual is a declaration: *This matters. I matter. My future is worth tending to today.*

Here's how to build one:

Light a candle and speak your dream out loud.

Play a song that stirs your courage.

Journal a sentence starting with "I am becoming the person who..."

End the week by celebrating progress rather than perfection.

Make the ritual yours. Make it joyful.

Even two minutes a day will remind you: *You're in it.*

Dream Activation Exercise: A Month of Bold Action

Dreams don't bloom someday.

They come alive in the *now*.

Choose one bold, aligned action each week for a month.

Week 1 – *Who do I need to become to bring this dream to life?*

Week 2 – *What conversation am I avoiding that could open new doors?*

Week 3 – *What fear am I ready to face and move through?*

Week 4 – *What small win would prove to me that I'm in motion?*

Each action is a match.

Keep striking, and the fire will catch.

Dream Detours: What To Do When You Fall Off Track

Every bold dreamer falls off track.

You'll have days when you question everything. When the fear feels louder than the dream.

That doesn't mean you've failed. To question, to fear, is to be human. What matters is getting *back* into alignment.

Here's a simple reset:

1. Pause. Breathe.
2. Ask: *What does my dream need from me right now?*
3. Take one tiny step.

The detour may actually deepen your commitment. Because returning to your dream, again and again, *builds belief*.

Dream Toolbox: Stay Aligned and Energized

Here are the tools I keep close for my bold dream journey:

- Dream Journal – Capture ideas, breakthroughs, and fears. Dreams love to be witnessed.

- Accountability Partner – Share your weekly action steps with a friend who believes in you.

- Bold Dream Board – Add not just images, but also words, quotes, *feelings*.

- "I Am Becoming" Affirmations – Speak who you're becoming before you fully believe it.

- Recovery Ritual – When you fall off track, have a go-to ritual that brings you back.

Pause & Reflect: Owning the Transformation

Get your journal. Ask yourself:

- When did I last surprise myself with courage?
- What dream am I secretly afraid *will work* and change everything?
- What part of me is finally ready to come alive?

This isn't just about achievement.

It's about *becoming*.

The Dream Reclaimed: After the Transformation

When you say yes to your dream, really yes, something inside clicks into place.

You feel it in your body.

In how you walk into a room.

In the decisions you make with clarity instead of confusion.

You begin to attract aligned opportunities because your energy says *I'm ready*.

You start hearing things like:

"You're glowing."

"Something's different about you."

Because something is. You're living in integrity with your dream.

And joy?
It becomes *fuel*.

Fuel for the Fire: Words to Carry You

"You may not control all the events that happen to you, but you can decide not to be reduced by them." [8]

—Dr. Maya Angelou

"Everything negative, pressure, challenges, is all an opportunity for me to rise." [9]

—Kobe Bryant

"Courage starts with showing up and letting ourselves be seen." [10]

—Brené Brown

"Your dream doesn't come to life the moment you get there, it starts the moment you decide you're worthy of it."

—Unknown

Let these quotes remind you of who you are.

Final Thoughts: This Is What Happens After

This chapter is about the after.

---

8 Maya Angelou, *Letter to My Daughter* (Random House, 2008), xii.

9 Kobe Bryant, quoted in Chris Ballard, "The Genius of Kobe Bryant," *Sports Illustrated*, May 2014

10 Brené Brown, *Daring Greatly: How the Courage to Be Vulnerable Transforms the Way We Live, Love, Parent, and Lead* (Gotham Books, 2012), 49

After the decision…

After the bold step…

After the fear…

comes something beautiful:

The quiet confidence of someone who trusts themselves.

The joy of living in alignment with what matters.

The momentum that builds when you stop looking back.

You'll wake up differently.

Move differently.

Speak with power.

Dream even bigger.

You do more than dream bold.

You live bold. You love bold. You lead bold.

This is what happens when you go all-in.

So, let's go.

Be bold. Be joyful. Be all-in.

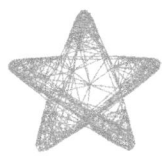

CHAPTER 9

BECOMING THE DREAM

There's something sacred about the moment you realize your dream is who you are becoming. I didn't understand that at first. I thought dreams were boxes to check, milestones to reach, outcomes to chase.

But becoming the dream? That's a whole different journey. That's about identity. Integration. Radiance. And it's where the magic lives.

> ★ **Wake-Up Call**
> When you become the dream, you change *everything*.

The Final Pause

You've done the work.

You've shed the old stories, the smallness, the fear.
And now, here you are
Standing at the edge of something undeniable.

Pause.
Breathe.
Smile.

This moment is quiet but full.
You're not who you were.
You're not pretending anymore.
This is the final breath before the leap,
the last heartbeat before the yes.
Not to a new role or title—
but to *you*.
To the self that has always been waiting to be claimed.
You said yes.
And everything changed.

A Moment of Becoming

"Events change lives." [11]

—Afrin Huq

I was sitting in a workshop about creative messaging, sharing my story, and holding space for dreamers. After the session, the woman sitting at the other end of the table slid over to me and said, "Thank you. You didn't just talk about the dream. You *are* the dream."

I froze. That sentence landed like truth. Because I wasn't performing. I wasn't pretending. I wasn't pitching. I was just *being*.

---

11 Afrin Huq, Stand Out & Thrive (event, September 2018)

Sometimes, the becoming process leads to an unexpected, profound change in identity. One you weren't looking for but showed up like a big concrete block.

At the Gross Global Happiness Summit at the University of Peace in Costa Rica, there was another such moment.

During a meditation toward the end of the event, something unexpected happened: A name appeared. *Kiran.*

I wasn't searching for a new name, but in that moment of stillness, it arrived with clarity and purpose. In Hindi and Sanskrit, Kiran means *ray of light*, a reminder of the dreams I nurture, the movement I'm building, and the transformation I'm embracing.

Afrin's words kept echoing in my mind: *Events change lives.* This one certainly did.

I had become the dream.

> ★ **Wake-Up Call**
> When you embody the dream, people *feel* it. Your presence speaks before you do. Your alignment creates its own gravity. You become a living invitation for others to dream again, too.

Rewriting the Narrative

A Parable

Once upon a time, there was a young man who started each day by going to his mirror to set his intentions for the day. This morning was just like any other morning.

The sun was up, the birds were chirping, and the upstairs neighbor's radio was blasting Wham's "Wake Me Up Before You Go-Go."

Actually, there was one thing that made this morning different. Today was his thirtieth birthday.

Unlike many of his friends, he looked forward to turning thirty. He was excited by what was to come and open to all the new experiences it would bring. He was starting the year off big. Not with a party, but a job interview.

He'd received a call earlier that week. His potential employers wanted to fly him down to meet with the team. He would need to come down the night before, and all his expenses would be covered. Airfare, hotel, car, food. Everything! He said yes, and for the next two days, he pinched himself to make sure he wasn't dreaming.

That is what went through his mind when he stepped up to the mirror this morning. With eyes closed, he took three deep breaths. Just as he finished, his cat jumped onto the sink and rubbed against his arm. "Silly cat," he said, and with a huge grin on his face, he looked into the mirror.

"Happy Birthday, and may all your dreams come true!"

The cat screeched, leapt off the sink, and knocked over the toothbrush and cup. Then, the image in the mirror began to speak.

"Sweetheart, dreams come after duty. You don't just chase what you want; you earn it. First, you be good. You be helpful. You do what's expected. Put others first. Don't make a fuss. Don't be selfish. Work hard. Stay late. Be the one they can count on. Smile, even when it hurts. That's how people will love you. That's how you'll matter. Your dreams? Those can wait. You have responsibilities now."

The story could have ended there. He could have picked up his toothbrush, brushed his teeth, finished his lukewarm coffee, and gone about his business, having an unremarkable birthday doing what he thought he had to do.

But not today. There must have been some pixie dust still lingering from the call he got two days ago, asking him to come in for an interview for the Walt Disney Company. And the magic of this being his birthday. Whatever it was, he felt bold something rise within him.

He went back to the mirror and, with new fire in his voice, challenged what he had just heard.

"But what if that's not true? What if I don't have to earn my worth by disappearing into everyone else's needs? What if being good doesn't mean being small? What if smiling through the pain is silence, not strength? What if love doesn't have to cost me my dream? What if I was never meant to wait? What if I already matter, just as I am? And what if the most responsible thing I could do... is to listen to the part of me that dares to want more?"

For the first time, he saw the difference between the life he was taught to live—and the life he was meant to live. So, he sat down and wrote out all the rules he'd been following. Not rules he chose, but rules he inherited. Absorbed. Obeyed. Then he rewrote them.

The Old Rule	My New Truth
Be helpful, not too ambitious.	I am allowed to want more.
Be nice, not too loud.	I am allowed to use my full voice.
Be supportive, not too visible.	I am allowed to take up space.
Don't make others uncomfortable.	I am allowed to challenge what no longer fits.
Stay safe, stay small.	I am allowed to be bold and take risks.
Wait your turn.	I am allowed to start now.
Prove yourself before you dream.	I am allowed to dream first.
Other people come first.	I am allowed to choose myself.

That list changed his life. Rewriting those rules meant *returning* to his authentic voice.

This revised list enabled him to begin *becoming* the person who could live his dream. And what came next? Joy. Light. Love. Because he was *coming home to himself*.

And that?

That was the best birthday gift I could've asked for.

Living As Revolution

"Just me existing, as an openly Black transgender woman from a working-class background, thriving, is a political act." [12]

—Laverne Cox

Becoming the dream often means claiming the truth of who you already are. Simply existing *as ourselves* is radical. Living your truth in a world that often asks you to blend in is one of the most revolutionary things you can do.

When you embrace your whole identity, including your dreams, with joy and pride, you make space for others to do the same. Your presence becomes their permission— your thriving as a form of resistance, which becomes their challenge of limiting beliefs. Your joy becomes a beacon that lights their path.

And that is more than enough to change the world.

---

12 Laverne Cox, interview by Michel Martin, *NPR*, June 29, 2014.

DREAMER SPOTLIGHT: DR. MAYA ANGELOU

(Poet, Author, Civil & Human Rights Activist)

A Life of Impact

. . . .

"If you're always trying to be normal, you will never know how amazing you can be." [13]

—Dr. Maya Angelou

Dr. Maya Angelou *embodied* truth. A legendary poet, memoirist, performer, and civil rights activist, she became one of the most powerful voices in American history. Her work spanned over fifty years, influencing generations with her unflinching honesty, lyrical prose, and unwavering commitment to truth, justice, and love.

She was the author of more than thirty published works, including poetry, essays, and autobiographies, most notably her groundbreaking memoir *I Know Why the Caged Bird Sings* published in 1969, which brought the realities of Black womanhood into mainstream literature with an unapologetic voice. She received over fifty honorary degrees and was awarded the Presidential Medal of Freedom, the nation's highest civilian honor.

Dr. Angelou was a literary giant, a teacher, a mentor, and a light for millions across the world. Her life was a testimony to the idea that who you are and how you live *is* your legacy.

---

13   Maya Angelou, quoted in Marcia Ann Gillespie, Rosa Johnson Butler, and Richard A. Long, eds., *Maya Angelou: Reflections* (New York: Bantam, 2004).

Dr. Angelou's early life was marked by trauma and silence. She stopped speaking for nearly five years after experiencing violence as a child. But even in that silence, her imagination was loud.

She wrote. She read. She observed.

Her voice returned, and powerfully.

She didn't emerge as a poet, performer, and activist overnight. She worked as a singer, dancer, journalist, and civil rights worker. Each chapter added depth to her becoming.

Her breakthrough came with *I Know Why the Caged Bird Sings*. This autobiographical work detailed her early life experiences with trauma, racism, and identity, and it was one of the first widely read books by a Black woman that tackled such themes with unflinching honesty. It was revolutionary in both content and voice: powerfully lyrical, deeply personal, and unapologetically Black and female. The book gave voice to the voiceless and helped countless readers find their own truth and resilience through her words.

Suddenly, the world recognized what Dr. Angelou had already accepted: Her life, her truth, her words, *mattered*.

She lived creativity. She showed us that every story has the power to heal, to connect, to free. She taught us that language can be both resistance and liberation.

Rather than chasing legacy, she *became* legacy by showing up as herself.

Even after fame, Dr. Angelou remained grounded in service.

She mentored generations. She stood on stages with presidents. She held space for joy and pain in the same breath.

Her dream was one about *significance*.

That's what it means to become the dream: to live in a way that echoes beyond your lifetime.

She left us with poems, books, speeches, but more than that, she left us with *permission*. To dream. To speak. To shine. To live fully and fiercely, as only we can.

Becoming Is Ongoing

Every bold choice, every small action, every quiet act of courage, shapes your identity. Your dream isn't something you achieve and walk away from. It's something you expand into. And as you grow, the dream grows with you. Think of it like a tree, rooted in your values, fueled by your actions, shaped by your story. It reflects who you are and who you're becoming.

But more than that, it guides you. It calls you to live with intention, to speak your truth even when your voice shakes, to choose joy when fear is easier, to be fully, unapologetically *you*.

The dream doesn't end once you reach the goal. In fact, that's when it begins to evolve.

You'll outgrow old dreams. You'll make space for new ones. You'll revisit old parts of yourself and reclaim them in new ways.

Becoming the dream means allowing yourself to change. To rise. To deepen. To return. And to do it with joy. With wonder. With your whole heart.

You don't owe the world a static version of yourself. You owe yourself a life that feels true. So grow. Shift. Expand. Celebrate.

The dream is alive in you. And it's just getting started.

Dream Activation Exercise: Write Your Dream Declaration

This is your declaration.

Take ten to fifteen minutes. Write a short personal declaration that affirms:

- Who you are becoming.

- What your dream means to you.

- How you will live in alignment with it.

Here's a prompt to get you started:

I am becoming someone who…

I believe my dream is…

I will honor my vision by…

Make it messy. Make it honest. Make it *yours*.

Hang it where you can see it. Let it remind you: The dream lives *in* you.

And that the life you're dreaming of… is already dreaming of *you*.

Dream Activation: Creating Your Dream Declaration

Before you write your declaration, take a moment to embody the dream. Not as a goal you're chasing, but as a life you're already living. This exercise is about identity, who you are when the dream is real.

Close your eyes. Take a breath. Feel it in your bones. Then complete the prompts below. Let your imagination speak. Let your future self speak. Let your dream speak.

This is your truth without filters. Let it flow.

Exercise 1: I Am... Step into the Dream

This is your invitation to step into the version of you who is already living the dream, not someday, but now. Close your eyes if you like. Take a breath. And complete the sentences below without overthinking. Let your dream speak through you.

I am...

(Who are you in your dream life? Describe yourself in the present tense.)

I am _____.

I am the kind of person who _____.

I am surrounded by _____.

I am known for _____.

I feel...

(How does living your dream feel in your body, mind, and spirit?)

I feel _____.

I awaken each day with _____.

I move through my life with _____.

I create...

(What are you building, making, or contributing?)

I create _____.

I bring _____ into the world.

I use my gifts to _____.

I receive...

(Let yourself imagine the rewards, both seen and unseen.)

I receive _____.

I welcome _____.

I allow myself to be supported by _____.

I am becoming...

(This is your ongoing evolution, what you're stepping into even more deeply.)

I am becoming _____.

I am claiming _____.

I trust that _____.

Take a moment to reread what you wrote. Is there a phrase that gives you chills or makes your heartbeat faster? Circle it. That's your dream calling.

Dream Activation Exercise 2: Create a Dream Daily Ritual

Dreams need care. A simple daily ritual helps you stay connected to your vision, especially when life gets loud.

Choose one or more of the following to build your own ritual. Keep it short, simple, and sacred:

- Say your **"I Am" identity** aloud each morning.
- Light a candle and ask: "What does my dream need from me today?"
- Write down one way your actions today moved you closer to your dream.
- Whisper your dream to yourself like a prayer.

Your dream is alive. Treat it like something sacred, because it is.

Final Thoughts: Live the Dream

This isn't a someday fantasy.

This is a *now* moment.

Your dream isn't just a vision board or a to-do list.

It's a way of *being*.

A way of *loving*. A way of *showing up*. A way of *shining*.

And every time you choose integrity over approval, curiosity over fear, alignment over convenience, you are becoming it.

You are no longer waiting to live the dream.
You *are* the dream.
You are the proof that becoming is possible.
So, live it out loud.
With joy. With grace. With fire.
Let the world feel the dream through your presence.
Let your life become the evidence.
Be the dream. And let it light the way for others.

"You're not done. You're unfolding."

—Kiran

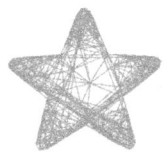

CLOSING WORDS

THE DREAM LIVES IN YOU

We began this book with a pause.

A moment to breathe.

To listen.

To remember what it feels like to want something more.

We didn't rush into dreaming. We slowed down enough to hear the whisper that's always been with you. The one that says, "This matters. You matter."

And now, here you are.

You've answered the questions.

You've met your doubt and reclaimed your power.

You've learned to take small steps, survive the messy middle, and build your dream with boldness and grace.

You've discovered that you don't just have a dream; you are the dream.

This is the becoming.

Not a finishing line.

Not a destination.

But a return to yourself.

Because your dream isn't a someday fantasy. It's a now identity.

A way of being.

A way of showing up.

And the world needs your dream lived out loud.

So,

Take one more breath.

Place your hand on your heart.

And say it, not for me, but for you:

I am ready.

Ready to trust the whisper.

Ready to take the next bold step.

Ready to live as the dream.

You don't need to wait for permission anymore. You've already given it.

Now it's time to begin again,

As the dream.

Welcome home.

Courage isn't chasing the dream.
It's saying yes to the life it's been dreaming for you.

—Kiran

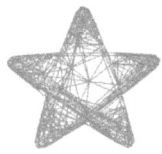

ACKNOWLEDGMENTS

Dreams aren't meant to be chased. They're meant to be lived. Living a dream this big, this personal, took more than just me.

Timm, thank you for dreaming right alongside me and for saying yes without always knowing the how. You are my anchor, my partner, my home. Your love and steadiness give me space to dream boldly and make it possible for me to keep saying yes. I wouldn't trade this life for anything.

Zelia, my boldest dream come true. You are my daughter, my teacher, my forever inspiration. Your courage, creativity, and fierce heart remind me why any of this matters. You carry the light of those who came before you and the spark of what's yet to be. Always remember: "Sing out, Louise!"

Davina, your yes made my biggest dream possible. Full stop. You opened the door, held the vision with me, and never let go. I'll never stop being grateful that you believed in the dream right from the start.

To the ones who helped shape this into something real
Anne Bartolucci, Tara Hayes, and Asya Blue, my creative collaborators, co-dreamers. My dream team. Thank you.

Anne, you helped me find the bones and the soul of this book. Your guidance shaped what it became.

Tara, you brought rhythm and clarity to every line. Your edits and proofreading helped the words breathe and settle into their truest form.

Asya, your design gave this project its visual heartbeat. You made it feel real and beautiful and whole.

Together, you turned my vision into something tangible that I could share with others.

To those who saw me more clearly than I saw myself.
Afrin, my friend, my coach, my partner in impact, and my inspiration. You saw me, you heard me. You gave me the courage to speak my stand and stand in my dream. Thank you for every nudge, challenge, cheer, and for being a sacred witness to it all.

To my grandparents, Fred and Bernice Baugh (in loving memory). This is your legacy. You lived the power of dreaming and passed it on. You showed me what it means to dream with faith, work with purpose, and love with your whole heart. Your example continues to be the wind beneath my wings, the roots beneath my dreams, and the whisper that still says, "Keep going." I carry you in everything I do.

To my mother, Hazel Marie Peach (in loving memory). I thank you for teaching me how to live with joy, lead with love, and dream without apology. Your love surrounds me still. You modeled what it means to show up with heart. You made beauty out of the ordinary, turned strangers into family, and believed in my dreams before I could even name them. This book carries your fingerprints. Every sunflower, every story, every risk I took to share this is because of the way you lived. I carry your light with me. Always.

To the communities who walked with me

To the HERD, Dreamers' Den, and The Alchemist's Pen Dreaming with you made this book possible. Your presence, encouragement, and shared vision carried me through the hard parts and cheered me through the breakthroughs.

You prove that dreaming is not a solo act. Thank you for walking with me and creating a safe space where bold visions could take root.

To you, the one holding this book in your hands.

You picked up this book for a reason you may not fully understand yet. Trust that whisper. There's a dream waiting for you. Say yes. You don't have to do it alone.

To the one I used to be.

You started this book as Kevin—heart full, vision clear, but not yet fully home to yourself.

Thank you for being brave enough to begin. For listening to the whisper. For putting words on a page when it was hard to speak them aloud. This book became the bridge you built.

And I crossed it to become Kiran. Thank you for starting. I've got it from here.

With love, memory, and a million dreams, thank you.
Kiran Baugh Ryan-Young

DREAMER SPOTLIGHT: KIRAN RYAN-YOUNG
(Author)

. . . .

"Dreams never fail."

–Kiran

They might not take the shape you expected. They might ask more of you than you thought you could give. But every true dream, when answered, will change you.

That's the kind of dreaming Kiran Ryan-Young lives for. The kind that doesn't just lead to achievement, but to transformation.

Born in Philadelphia and currently living in Bedford-Stuyvesant, Brooklyn, Kiran came to New York as an actor, chasing roles and applause. But the more he listened, the more he felt drawn to something quieter, deeper. He realized that the real stage, the one that mattered, was the space you created for someone else to finally say: Here's what I really want.

That instinct was planted early. His mother, Hazel, believed in dreaming out loud. Paris was her favorite place in the world, and she returned to it often, as if it called her back to herself. From Hazel, Kiran learned that dreaming is a sacred birthright and that travel is one way we remember who we are.

Then Zelia arrived, and nothing was abstract anymore. Becoming "Papa" gave Kiran's dream a heartbeat. Legacy took on new meaning. Presence became the truest measure of success.

Somewhere between the wisdom his mother left behind and the wonder his daughter awakened, Kiran made a choice. He shed the name he'd been given—William Kevin Young—and stepped fully into one that felt like truth: *Kiran*, meaning ray of light. *Baugh*, his mother's name, to carry her lineage forward. *Ryan-Young* to root him in the family he's continuing to build.

The name change was a commitment. A declaration of becoming.

That's what Kiran helps others do now: become.

He's spent his life helping people turn whispers into words, and words into movement. Whether through theater, entrepreneurship, or personal transformation, his work is always the same: honor the dream, create the space, walk the path with others.

Through **A Million Dreamers**, Kiran creates spaces where bold visions take root and grow. He hosts **Dreamers' Den** circles—gatherings where people pause, reflect, and speak their dreams aloud—and leads **Permission to Dream**, a signature event that invites participants to reconnect with possibility. His body of work includes courses, workshops, journals, rituals, and an oracle-style **card deck for visionaries**, all designed to keep dreamers moving with clarity and care.

He was a co-founder of **Carousel Theatre Company**, where creative expression and community storytelling took center stage, and launched **Synergy Squared Inc.** with his husband, **Timm**, to help creatives and entrepreneurs build the systems they need to turn big ideas into sustainable momentum.

The practices in this book are more than theories; they're lived experience:

The Pause, to hear what's true.

Bold dreams, simple steps, to stay grounded.

The messy middle, where fear and magic coexist.

And always, the return to a core belief:

You are not behind. You are becoming.

If this book is in your hands, trust that it's not by accident. Your next version is calling. The dream has already begun its work.

So take a breath.

Place your hand on your heart.

And remember:

Dreams never fail.

They change you. And that's everything.

YOUR DREAM
JOURNEY CONTINUES

Wake Up! It's Time to Dream invites you to see what's possible—**The Time to Dream Collection** helps you live it. Turning the last page is not the end—it's an awakening. That's why I created this companion: to help you carry the vision beyond these words and into your everyday life.

Each piece inside has been chosen to spark inspiration, guide reflection, and remind you that dreams don't fade—they wait for you to claim them. Consider it your next step, a way to keep becoming the dream you are meant to be.

You can discover the collection at www.TimeToDream.co.

Because your dream isn't a fantasy—it's a future with your name on it.